Decoupage

DECOUPAGE

Refurbish your home using paper, glue and scissors

Sandra Nunes

Pasija-Art

Decoupage
Refurbish your home using paper, glue and scissors

Author
Sandra Nunes

Graphic Design
Denis Rakarić

Proof reader
Ljiljana Drnić

Translated by
Korana Lovrić

Photos
Danijela Gotal Grgurač i
Dalibor Gotal

Publisher
Pasija-Art

ISBN 978-1490321998

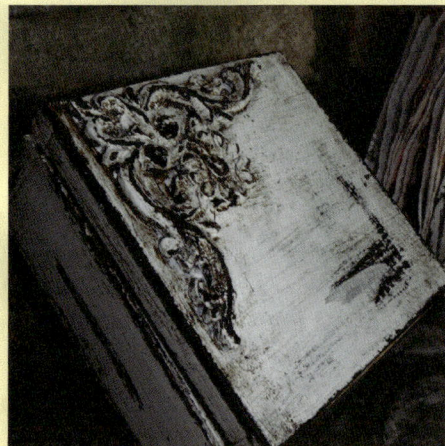

„*If you want to do nothing, fall in love with what you're doing*"

Jonathan Swift

Contents

Projects

I thank my sons Andro and Niko for their patience, love and understanding during the emergence and creation of my first book on decoupage, which is a result of an unexpected love and passion for decoupage, for the art of creating and decorating items that make our interior space. Interior space – that's our home, and home is where the heart is ... it is an emotion that reflects us and shows who we are. It indicates our lifestyle ... like what our selection of books, movies or music says about us...

I thank my parents, brother Marko and his girlfriend Sanja, as well as all my friends for their constant support and encouragement.

Special thanks to Fabio, my great friend who first spotted my talent and love for art creation and who perceived my passion for decoupage, maybe even before I did. It was enough that someone just pointed out the point in me which makes me happy and joyful. I thank him for his vision and faith in me. With his help, I turned my dream into reality... and I'm still living it...

I thank all very talented and charming people who were in any way involved in the preparation of this book .... my mom Ljiljana Drnić who made my sentences fluent and understandable; Denis Rakarić who graphically designed the book and prepared a wonderful layout for over a hundred of my photos; Danijela Gotal Grgurač, graphic designer, and her father Dalibor Gotal, artist and photographer from Sisak, who turned my work into a playful vintage magic with his sharp eye of a photographer...

And finally, thanks to Sona Šuhajdova, my teacher and mentor, who taught me everything I know and whose works are my inspiration ... I admire Sona as a woman and as a talented artist...

Sandra Nunes

Introduction to Decoupage

Welcome to the wonderful world of decoupage ...

Decoupage is the art and the skill of decorating by cutting out motifs or pictures from paper, which originated in France and Venice in the 18th century. The word itself comes from the French verb "découper", which means "to cut out" and apply, usually on three-dimensional objects. The basic principle is simple: select the appropriate image, carefully cut it out, paste it onto the prepared surface, and then complete the project with several layers of varnish. Decoupage is also called the napkin technique because napkins and various decoupage papers are very often used while decorating.

The art of decoupage has undergone a revival in recent years, due to the availability of an abundance of printed material. However, decorating using cut out motifs and images for decorative purposes exists for centuries. Such kind of decorating was first developed in China, around 105 BC, and then in Europe, in the 12th century.

Decoupage appeared in Italy in the second half of the 17th century and was a very popular pastime for women of that era. During the 1800s and after the development of advanced printing techniques, high-quality prints were produced in large quantities. This printed material was called "scrap". In Victorian times in the UK, this kind of decorating using images and motifs for decorative purposes was readily used, and decoupage became a favourite hobby. Such kind of production has experienced a commercial success, and today a revival.

For those who are new to this skill, decoupage offers an excellent means of creative expression. The only requirements are patience, enthusiasm and an eye for colour. With relatively little effort, you can turn almost every humble household object into a genuine work of art. Whether it is a large or small surface.... you can breathe new life into each one. Jewellery, a picture frame, a vase, a toy box, even the walls and doors, almost everything can be decorated with decoupage. After overcoming the initial obstacles in learning this skill, only one problem remains, and that is to know when to stop ... all decoupage enthusiasts will agree...

How to Use This Book?

The aim of the book "Decoupage – with paper, glue and scissors" is to familiarize the reader with this interesting technique of decorating, using a two-stage system to create elegant decoupage projects.

In each of the ten inspiring lessons, the first phase shows a decoupage technique - overall there are five - and then in the second phase, always through two projects, it is shown how the afore mentioned and described techniques can be imaginatively incorporated in the wonderful process of creating decoupage. Such comprehensive volume of a rounded gallery of projects can intrigue and inspire a still undiscovered decoupage artist in you too...

Getting Started

This section covers everything you'll need to get started with various projects. Don't worry, you won't have to buy everything at once, so you don't blow a hole in your household budget for the following few months! Certain necessary accessories needed for most of the projects can, if used correctly, be used for a long time over and over again. If you already have experience with decoupage, you'll have a pretty good idea about the listed items, and if not, just carefully read the particular section to see what's needed.

It's always tempting to ignore parts of a book, such as this introductory chapter, and immediately start the project, but if you've come this far, I recommend you read everything because I included a number of new ideas and practical advice.

Basic Materials

Which materials can we decoupage???

All objects made from untreated or raw wood, varnished wooden surfaces, textile, glass, plastic, terracotta, porcelain, ceramic, stone, metal objects, cardboard and MDF, objects made from straw, candles, walls...

With all the new media available today there is really no limit to your creative expression when it comes to finding something on which the decoupage technique can be applied. From the smallest picture frame to decorating the entire wall, the only thing that can restrain you is your imagination. There are very few things that can give you so much pleasure as converting plain boxes or pieces of old furniture into works of art.

New Raw Wood

New raw wood is by far the most accessible source of basic materials. Bare wooden materials such as boxes, picture frames or wooden floors are a real blessing for decoupage enthusiasts. They don't require a lot of preparation, and most vendors have a great selection of items.

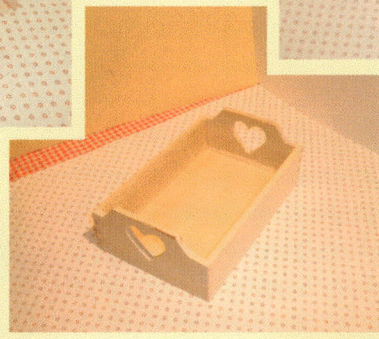

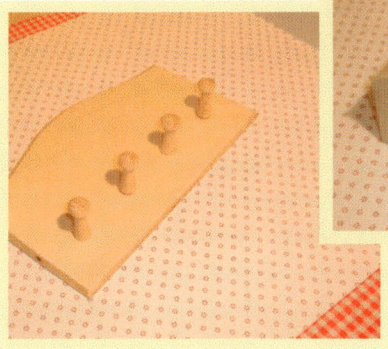

New Varnished Wood

If you want to work with new varnished wood, that is, you can't get this kind of material in its raw state; you can always buy items that have already been varnished. If you purchased a new varnished wood, it won't have too many layers of varnish and wax on it, so it won't be too difficult to remove varnish or wax from it. The reason for striping down to raw wood is you'll be using paint and water-based adhesives, which are incompatible with an oil-based varnish.

Old Wood and Metal

Old wood and metal make a great source of material for decorating because they are very special and impressive. Any such wooden or metal product is unique, which adds to its value. Unfortunately, the decoration process is preceded by a long preparation phase. Visit your attic, garage or local antiques fair, you'll be surprised with what you can find there. Old suitcases, bowls, boxes and cans... a treasure of discarded and forgotten items which can be transformed into genuine little works of art.

Ceramics

Ceramics are suitable for painting and decorating with the decoupage technique. Many items are available in arts and crafts stores or you maybe have a bunch of them at home too. Items decorated in this way are solely decorative ... used for storing nuts, Potpourri or the like. They are not to be used for serving hot food or even fruit, which may eventually create mildew and destroy the container. These items are purely decorative. Wipe them with a damp cloth, but do not immerse them in water or wash in a dishwasher.

Glass

Glass can also be used as a base for decoupage. It must be dry and thoroughly cleaned before decorating. All decorated glassware is mostly only decorative, as is the case with ceramic or porcelain...

Candles and Soaps...

Yes, you can decoupage them too!

But don't use candles that are too thin because the flame could reach the paper during burning. That's why it's better to decorate thick candles with the wick in the middle, not on the side.

Any soap can also be decoupaged, provided it's not too "oily". Decoupaged soaps are not necessarily purely decorative, that is, they can be used. The image will eventually fall off, disappear as the soap disappears, but that shouldn't worry you too much.

Accessories for Decoupage

Nowadays it's very easy to decorate furniture and many other objects using the decoupage technique. If you like decoupage, find a place for yourself and make your art. The essential accessories for the technique of decoupage are small and large scissors, scalpels, pens, cloths and sponges, flat synthetic brushes of different thickness, tweezers ... You also need to have larger and smaller containers for mixing colours. Do not forget different sanding papers, which are necessary for sanding wood surfaces or removing excess napkins.

As with any other type of handicraft production, it's essential to have adequate equipment for decoupage. Make sure that all the necessary equipment is arranged on the work surface before you begin the project.

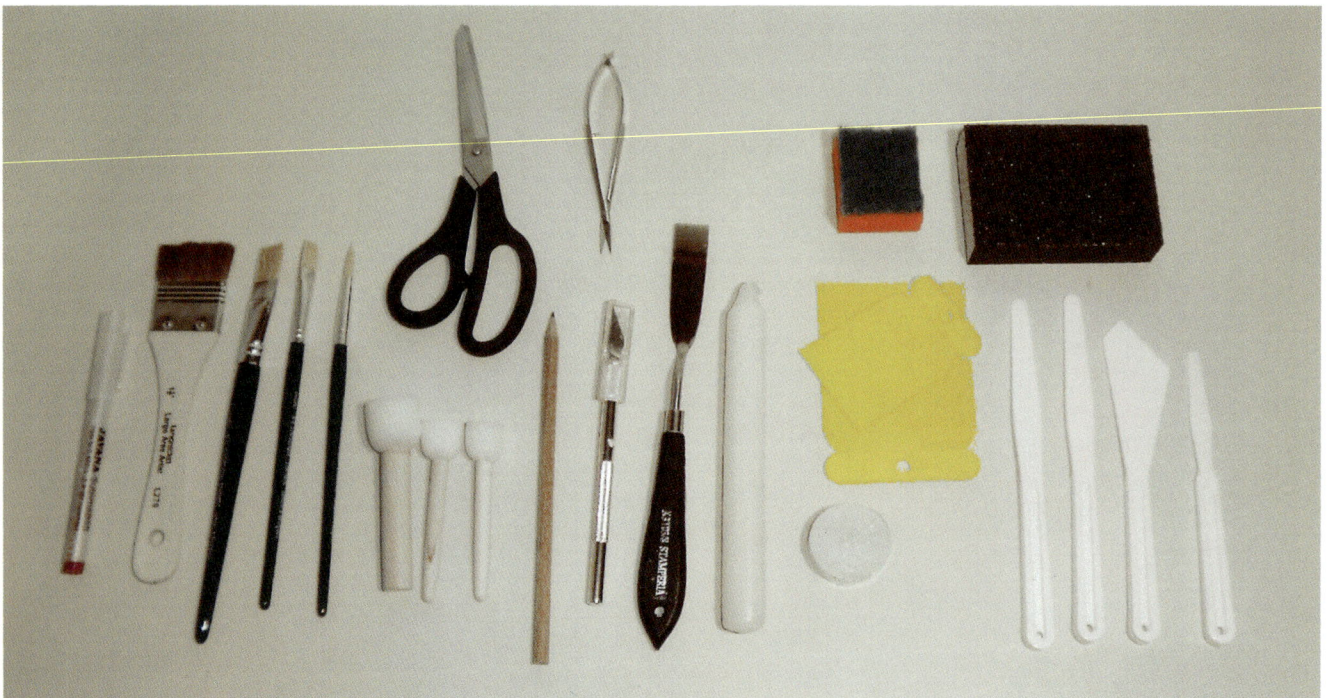

Scissors

Small pair of sharp scissors is very important for decoupage. Choose scissors which fit comfortably in your hand. Scissor blades can be straight or curved. Also always have a larger pair nearby for cutting excess paper before the final and more complex stage of cutting. Scissors should always be sharp and only be used for cutting paper.

Scalpel

Scalpels are perfect for detailed cutting, which is also included in the decoupage technique. There are scalpels with a rotating tip which are ideal for cutting out circles and small curved edges. Always have a spare scalpel, because cutting with a blunt instrument can ruin your paper motif.

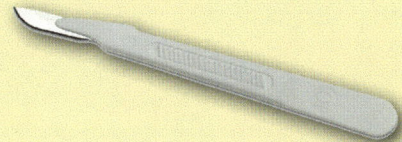

Self Healing Cutting Mat

Self healing cutting mat protects your work surface from being cut by scalpel, and is ideal for cutting classic decoupage papers.

Tweezers

Tweezers are used for grabbing tiny pieces of cut out paper and for use in three-dimensional decoupage.

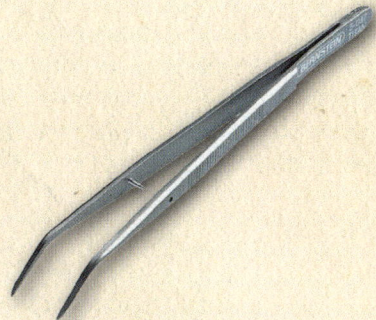

Sandpaper

Sandpaper (also called glass or emery paper) is used for surface treatment with a sander or by hand. There are different types of sandpaper, which is characterized by a different surface structure intended for treatment of wood, paint or metal. Sandpaper is divided into different so-called grit sizes, which are indicated by numbers and reflect on the impact of removal. In general: the smaller the grit size, the coarser the sandpaper and therefore the greater the removal.

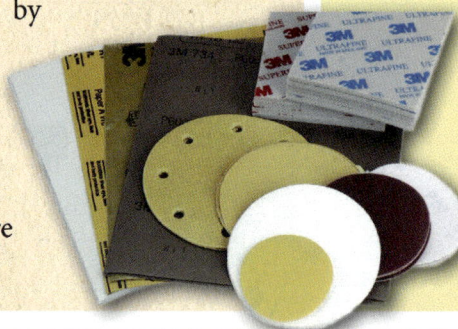

Ruler and Measuring Equipment

Transparent ruler is ideal for measuring and marking.

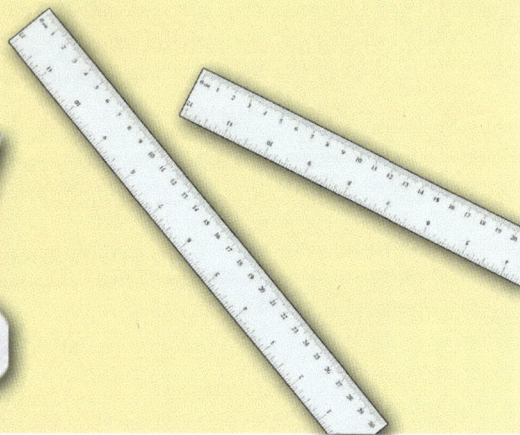

Brushes

A brush is one of the most important tools of your creative expression. Your work will quickly make you generate a collection of different brushes. It's important to have a variety of brushes, ranging from fine small brushes for colouring and shading to large and flat brushes which are used for general painting and varnishing.

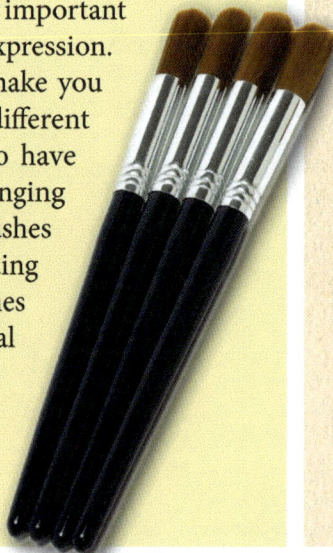

Brushes for thick paints such as oil or acrylic, are made with hog bristles and are usually flat. Denser colour requires a stiffer brush, which can be made from natural or synthetic filaments. A quality brush is the one whose bristles don't fall out and whose shape doesn't alter when working with it. There are flat, curved, pointed and fan-shaped brushes, and their size is determined by a number. A smaller number means a thinner brush; a larger number means a bigger, that is, a thicker brush. Brush sizes range from 0 – 40.

Varnishes, Wax, Paints...

Acrylic Paint

Acrylic paints are ideal for the decoupage technique ... Colours are water-based, with selected pigments, can be diluted with water and mixed. Acrylic paint can be applied in different ways, with a brush, sponge, fingers... Colours provide an excellent cover and are quick-drying, resistant to weather conditions on porous materials. They have a pleasant odour, can be used indoors and can be painted over.

Brushes and other supplies are rinsed with water.

Colours can be used in combination with various techniques and crackle varnishes.

They are ideal for the following surfaces: wood, paper, cloth, stone, metal, glass, clay, ceramics, wax, plastic, plaster, modelling pastes...

Varnish and Glue for Napkins

Napkin glue is a quick drying water-based medium, easy to use because of its 2 in 1 principle (the same product is used to glue and varnish the napkin), and it has no odour.

It's ideal for the following surfaces: wood, plaster, cardboard, plastic, terracotta, metal, polystyrene, stone ... and there are also various types - glossy, matte, sequined...

Brushes and other tools are rinsed with water, and after drying the varnish becomes water resistant.

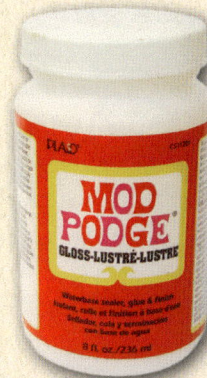

Crackle Varnish –Crackle Media

Using a crackle medium we can achieve an antique crackle effect. There are two basic crackle media - crackle varnish and two-component crackle varnish.

Crackle Varnish

This is a transparent water-based varnish used in combination with acrylic paint. It's applied to a surface which has previously been painted with acrylic paint. The varnish is best applied with a soft synthetic flat brush in one direction and in one stroke. Once the medium layer has dried (not completely, so that it's still a little wet to the touch after approx 30-45 min) a contrasting acrylic paint is applied, in the same direction in which we applied the medium. Cracks will appear during the drying process, depending on the coating thickness.

Therefore this medium is not used as the final medium on your decoupage picture. You can use it around your design or as a basis for a design, but not across it. Given that it is a water-based medium, the brush is rinsed with warm water and soap. [1]

Two-Component Crackle Varnish

There are two types of the two-component crackle varnish. One is water based - both components, while the other has a nitro-based and a water-based component. When it comes to cleaning brushes it's important to know which of the two types of media you're working with. For the water-based medium, clean the brush with warm water and soap, while the brush covered in a nitro-based component should be washed in turpentine.

Ideally use two brushes. What's particular about this medium is that it is applied over the finished work or, in case of a glass surface, before your motif.

The design becomes cracked, and in those cracks metallic powders, antique pastes, bitumen or oil paints are rubbed in. There are also media that are completely transparent and those that are yellowish, or antique. [2]

---

[1] Data on patination agents listed in the Section on Crackle Varnish –Crackle Media is taken from http://www.nb-net.hr/nbh3.php. (03.02.2013.).
[2] Data on patination agents listed in the Section on Crackle Varnish –Crackle Media is taken from http://www.nb-net.hr/nbh3.php. (03.02.2013.).

Patination agents

Patina comes in various shapes, but they all have a task of aging the objects we produce.

Patina adds a touch of the past which we love to see on our beloved objects and keeps them warm with the warmth of past events. Patina may be just what could give credibility to a picture frame in shabby chic style or age a chest decorated with crackle varnish for a couple of years.

Dark wax is another natural product that also protects the object in addition to giving a patina. Ideal for use on wood, gives a patina along with protection and a warm brown color highlighting the structure and the annual rings in the wood. Serves as patina, as protection, as a final layer or as an agent for rubbing into the cracks in two-component varnish.

Neutral wax is an ideal top coat for a beautiful satin sheen. If it's rubbed into wood, the wood gets care and protection. The wax is applied with a cloth and has a wonderful vanilla cream scent. Along with the protective function it can also be mixed with pigments. That is how we get patinas of different colours. Excellent effects are also achieved if wax is applied instead of candles in the shabby chic style.[3]

Patina is the favourite brown patina which gives objects a warm brown colour. It can serve as a stain, colouring wood without losing the wood structure, it can be placed on pittorico to soften transitions and age the surface, or it can be rubbed into cracks using two-component crackle varnish... Patina is alcohol-based and the brush is cleaned with alcohol. It's applied with a paper towel or a cloth.[4]

---

[3]Data on patination agents listed in the Section on Patination Agents is taken from http://www.lumos.hr/patina.htm. (09.02.2013.).
[4]Data on patination agents listed in the Section on Patination Agents is taken from http://www.lumos.hr/patina.htm. (09.02.2013.).

Structural Pastes

Structural pastes are divided into two groups: pastes and gels. High density acrylic pastes are used for 3D effects and to add structure in various techniques. Pastes are used for covering and after drying they become opaque while gels become transparent. All pastes are applied with a trowel or a plastic knife which are rinsed with water after use.

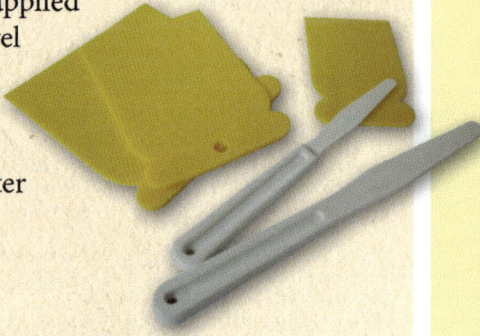

Paper

One of the most important and basic materials used for decoupage is paper with various motifs. Basic types of decoupage paper are: napkins, rice paper, decoupage classic paper, but something completely different can also be used. It depends on the creativity of the artist - some artists, for example, use dried flowers.

How to decoupage...????

Basic Napkin Decoupage Technique

Napkin technique is a very simple and popular technique which allows you to decorate various materials such as wood, clay flower pots, clay tiles, glass, paper or cardboard boxes, fabric, metal cans, candles, etc.

Decoupage is a favourite technique among creative people, probably because success is assured. If you are not skilled in artistic expression using a pen or a brush, master the napkin technique and you can create unique decorative items for your home...

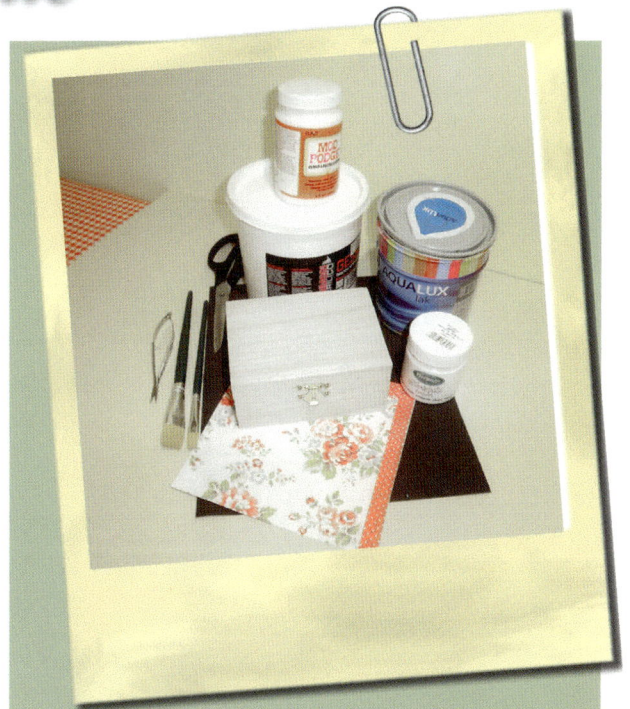

Materials

- Decoupage glue
- Transparent water-based varnish for the finishing coat
- Napkins of different patterns and colours
- Acrylic paints

Items for decorating

PVC balls and other pre-made forms of PVC, wooden objects, boxes, picture frames, terracotta pots, jars, candle holders, candles, roof shingles, Styrofoam shapes and pre-made forms, etc.

Surface Preparation

First start by preparing the base on which you will paste napkins.

Clean the object thoroughly.

Whether it's wood, metal, plastic, cardboard, glass or ceramic... regardless of the type of surface you choose, good preparation is the key to success.

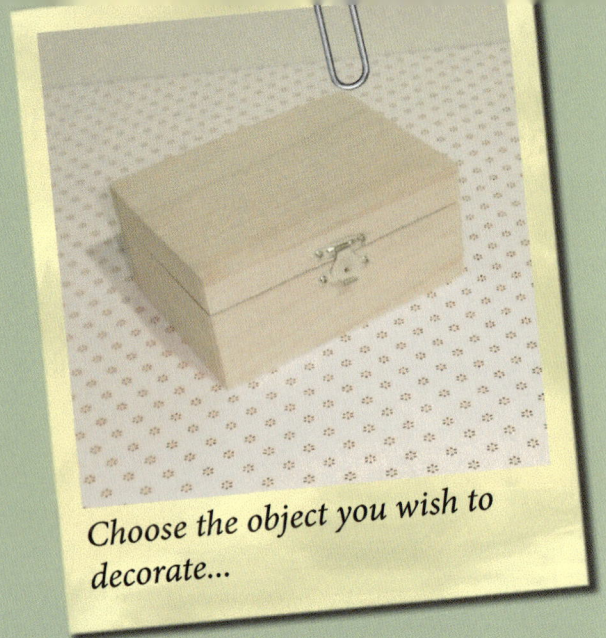

Choose the object you wish to decorate...

Accessories and materials

1 a wooden case
2 sandpaper
3 putty (if necessary, that is, if the wooden object is damaged)
4 a plastic knife
5 paper towels

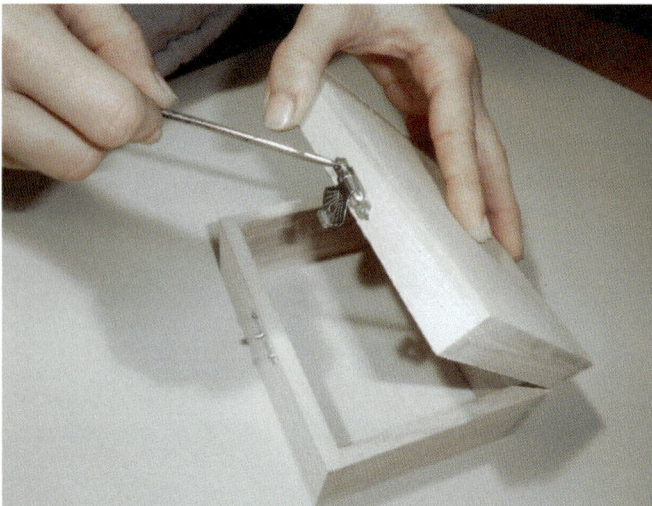

Step 1
Sand the wooden or painted surfaces with fine sandpaper (no. 600, 800, 1000). Wipe the dust and allow it to dry.

Step 2
Use putty for correcting holes, cracks, surface irregularities or bumps.

Step 3
When the putty dries, sand the surface again, wipe off the dust and let it dry.

Step 4
Touch the surface with your fingers and check if there are any irregularities. If so, sand all sharp edges or bumps again.

Step 5
When you are satisfied that the surface is perfectly smooth, use paper towels to wipe off any dust particles. Once the putty is completely dry, your wooden box will be ready for painting.

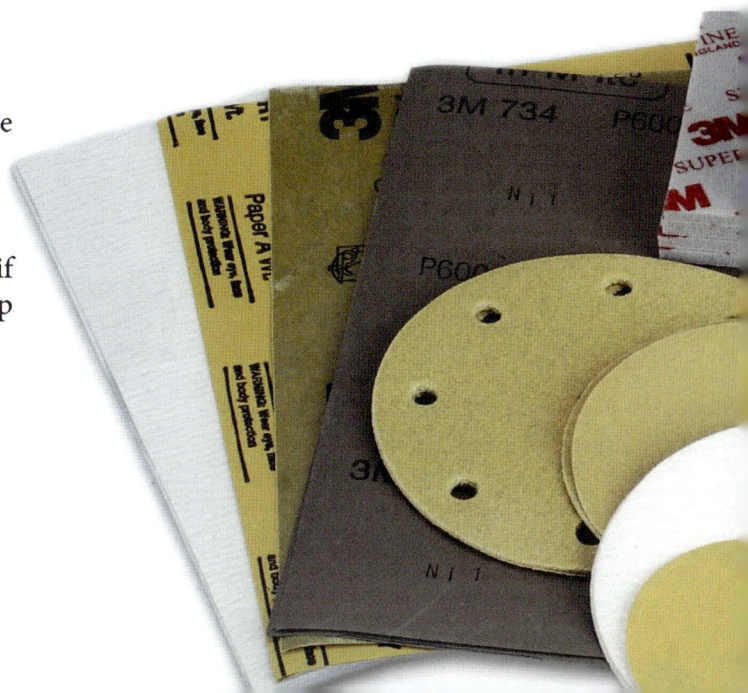

Painting

It's necessary to paint the object beforehand with white or another lighter shade of acrylic paint (a special acrylic palette of pastel colours in shades of vanilla, light pink, light yellow and ivory is available for this purpose...). Try to choose a colour which works well with the napkin. For example, if the napkin is yellow, select a soft yellow background.

Paint can be applied with a sponge or a brush. Once you paint the object, allow it to air dry thoroughly. Only then can we move on to applying the napkin.

TIP!
How to achieve warm pastel tones????

When you want to make a warm pastel tone by mixing acrylic paints, never use white acrylic for ivory or vanilla tones. White will give you cold light tones, and ivory will reward you with warm and pastel tones. For example, a little bit of ivory and green will give you a beautiful pastel olive, and if you mix white and green, you will get a cool light green colour. The same is true for red, blue and lilac colours.[7]

What if the background is dark?

When working on darker surfaces like wooden boxes, cardboard boxes, etc., the surface must be well prepared. If you want to paint, for example, a dark brown cardboard box yellow, you'll need to apply a very thick layer of paint to get the desired shade. The background colour will be visible through a thinner layer of the selected colour. A thick coat may break over time and destroy the work.[5]

The trick is in the preparation of the background with the white Gesso colour (example). Apply it in two thin layers; let each dry thoroughly and lightly sand using fine sandpaper. The surface will then be smooth and ready for any shade you want. If the surface is too absorbent, before applying Gesso, coat the surface with a thin layer of wood glue diluted with water to clog the pores of the surface, and dry thoroughly. When your desired shade has white colour as the base, like a shade of vanilla, Gesso can be applied in a single layer.[6]

---

[5]Data in the Section on Painting is taken from http://hobbyboom.blogspot.com/p/savjeti-i-trikovi.html. (20.02.2013.).
[6]Data in the Section on Painting is taken from http://hobbyboom.blogspot.com/p/savjeti-i-trikovi.html. (20.02.2013.).
[7]http://nbhobby.com/nbh7.php. (09.02.2013.).

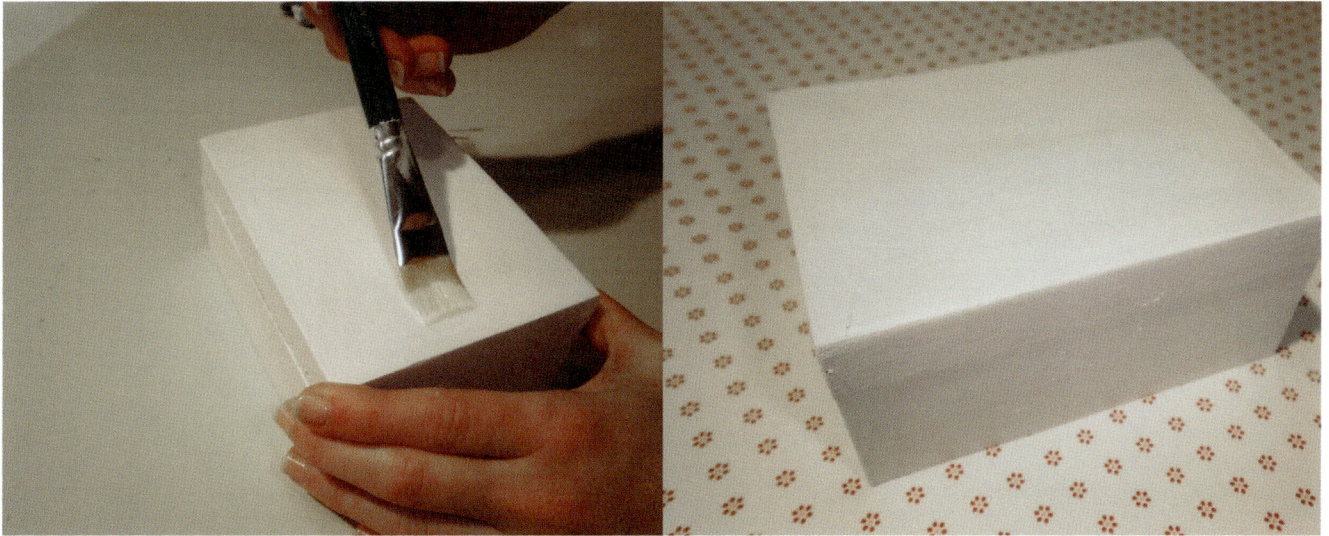

Step 1

Always first apply wood primer to a wooden object.

Step 2

After the primer, paint the object with acrylic paint. Background colour is extremely important in decoupage. It can stick out, but it can also contribute to the harmony of the whole work.

Apply one or two layers of the selected acrylic paint. Allow to dry.

Step 3

Once the paint is dry, sand lightly just to remove brush strokes, if you were working with a thick acrylic paint.

Applying the Napkin

Select the desired design on the napkin and cut. Napkins usually have 2 or 3 plies, and white layers should be separated before gluing, so that only the thin top layer of the napkin with the motif remains.

Gluing and fixing

Gluing the napkin

The place where the napkin or the motif will be glued is thinly coated with decoupage glue. The adhesive is applied with a brush.

Put the napkin motif on the glue while it's still wet and gently slide your fingers across the napkin from the centre to the ends until the napkin is aligned with the base. Then apply a layer of glue on the napkin using a flat brush. Be careful not to tear the napkin. Let it all dry.

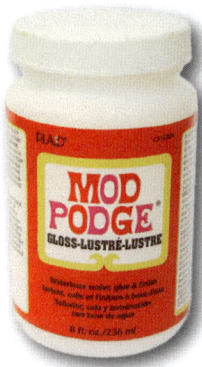

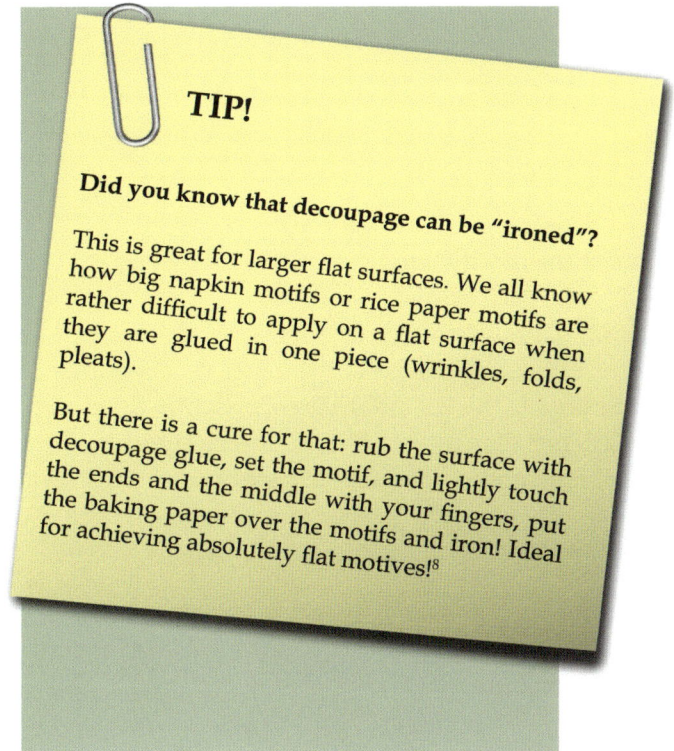

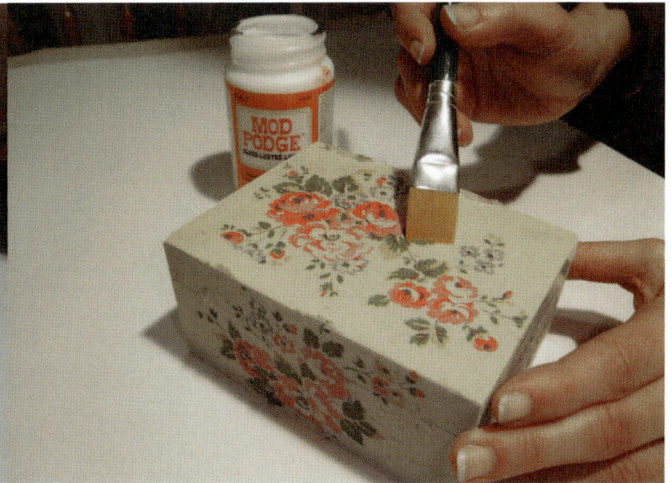

TIP!

Did you know that decoupage can be "ironed"?

This is great for larger flat surfaces. We all know how big napkin motifs or rice paper motifs are rather difficult to apply on a flat surface when they are glued in one piece (wrinkles, folds, pleats).

But there is a cure for that: rub the surface with decoupage glue, set the motif, and lightly touch the ends and the middle with your fingers, put the baking paper over the motifs and iron! Ideal for achieving absolutely flat motives![8]

[8]http://hobbychic.blogspot.com/2010/03/tipsn-tricks.html. (09.02.2013.).

Gluing the classic Decoupage Paper

Select the motif taking care not to mix styles.

Using slightly curved scissors carefully cut out the motifs. Cutting paper is the basis of decoupage. If the paper is thicker, hold scissors slightly tilted to the right. You can cut paper more precisely in that way. It's important to have a good pair of scissors, so don't use them on anything other than decoupage paper or napkins.[9]

TIP !

How to "thin" the edges of decoupage paper?

If you held scissors away from yourself while cutting paper, that is, tilted slightly to the right, you will not see the white edges of the paper. But if you do see them, try to remove them before gluing. This can be done by soaking the tip of a crayon in turpentine and tracing it over the edges of the white paper. They will disappear!![10]

Or

When the decoupage with classic paper is ready and dry, all outer edges of the surface can be sanded with fine sandpaper (300+ grit).[11]

[9]http://www.perlica.hr/hr/trgovina/74-decoupage-salvetna-tehnika.html?page=shop.browse&sef=c. (09.02.2013).
[10]http://www.perlica.hr/hr/trgovina/74-decoupage-salvetna-tehnika.html?page=shop.browse&sef=c. (09.02.2013.).
[11]http://www.nb-net.hr/nbh6.php. (09.02.2013.).

Step 1
Cut the appropriate design from the classic paper, put the motif onto a flat surface and arrange the imagined composition onto the object you're decorating. Follow the imagined composition and take care of the colours when you're arranging cropped motifs.

Step 2
When you are satisfied with the arrangement you created, take a phantom pen whose trace disappears after a while and draw a contour around the cut out motif. These contours are a guide for gluing.

Step 3
Take the chosen motif, apply a thin layer of glue on the back and glue it to a spot you've previously outlined.

TIP !

Pockets of air can always appear on the classic decoupage paper, while the glue or varnish is drying.

If despite all your efforts pockets of air appear on paper due to the lack of glue, take a scalpel with a sharp knife; make a thin cut on the decoupage paper in order to make the cut less noticeable.

Gently lift the paper and apply the adhesive with a toothpick into the cut part and press down with your fingers to glue it firmly.[12]

Step 4
Gently push the air away from the middle of the classic paper towards the edges using your fingers or a rubber spatula, making sure to flatten out any wrinkles at the same time, if they appeared during gluing.

Step 5
Apply a thin layer of glue over the classic paper too, using a brush.

Step 6
When you have finished gluing the cut out motifs, coat the entire decoupage piece with glue, even the parts where you didn't glue the paper motifs. Remove the excess adhesive using a paper towel. Allow it to dry completely.

[12]http://www.perlica.hr/hr/trgovina/74-decoupage-salvetna-tehnika.html?page=shop.browse&sef=c. (09.02.2013.).

Gluing Rice Paper

Rice paper is a thin, printed paper, ideal for the napkin technique. It's very similar to the napkin; it needs to be glued to light surfaces because of its transparency.

You don't need to cut it, just tear it up. It adapts perfectly to surfaces and is excellent in combination with conventional crackle varnish.

TIP !

When you want to separate a motif from the rice paper you can always use a pair of scissors. However, it's much easier to tear up the motif using fingers.

So that tearing would be even easier, gently circle the motif with a soft brush dipped in cold water and then slowly pull, and the motif will be ready for pasting.[13]

---

[13]http://www.lumos.hr/ideje.htm. (09.02.2013.).

Varnishing

Select the type of varnish you want to use. It can be glossy, matt or satin.

TIP !

If, while varnishing, a "Milky Way", appears on your project, that is because you have applied layers of varnish before the previous layer has dried enough.

Leave it be for two to three days and then sand everything with sandpaper and re-varnish.[14]

Step 1
When the glue is dry to the touch, varnish the whole piece with a thin layer of decoupage varnish. Allow it to dry well. Apply a second coat ... let it dry well and apply a third layer of varnish and allow to dry thoroughly.

Step 2
Sand the third layer of varnish with fine sandpaper for wood. Rub in one direction using slight pressure. In decoupage, sanding is as important as varnishing. Wipe the sanding dust with a dry cloth and varnish with another thin layer of lacquer.

---

[14]http://www.perlica.hr/trgovina/74-decoupage-salvetna-tehnika.html?page=shop.browse&sef=c. (09.02.2013.).

Drying

After drying, the object is water and weather resistant. Brushes are rinsed with water immediately after working with them and in short, that's it...

Projects

Phase 1: Technique

Shabby chic

Contrary to popular belief, shabby chic is not a technique but an effect. So, it's a few techniques which give new things a distressed, worn out look. Antique effect is achieved with the help of several techniques without crackle varnish; although it can be combined with two-component varnish for more delicate cracks.

1. The first step is to look for a decorative item that will be processed. It would be best if you found a piece of solid wood, which you will surely be able to find somewhere in your attic or basement. If you don't find it there, visit fairs where you can always find similar things cheaply.

2. Sand the object with fine sandpaper to remove all polish. This is necessary so that the next coat would adhere better and to make sure that all impurities are removed. After matting, go over with a piece of damp cloth to remove dust.

3. Paint the object with a dark acrylic paint or paint only the edges where you want to achieve the shabby effect.

4. When the paint is dry, rub the edges of the object with a plain white candle (paraffin), as well as all other spots from which you later want to scrape off the paint. Paraffin provides a layer of grease from which the acrylic paint will later be sanded off easier, leaving specific vintage patterns. Rub the edges and parts around the handles and worktops in particular.

3

4

5. Apply a layer of an opposite shade of acrylic paint and then let it dry. Apply the paint with a brush in the middle layer. It doesn't matter if traces of the brush remain, you will achieve a more antique look that way, and sandpaper will later smooth things out a little bit and lessen the brushstrokes.

6. Go over the object with sandpaper or a scalpel to remove the coat of paint applied over the paraffin - grease, which will create a pattern of a shabby item. Optionally, you can just gently take off the colour or by going over the same place multiple times create a stronger shabby effect.

7. If you wish, you can paste patterns from napkins or rice paper, and protect the whole object with varnish or matt napkin glue. If you want, you can apply two-component crackle varnish over the entire object for a cracked effect.

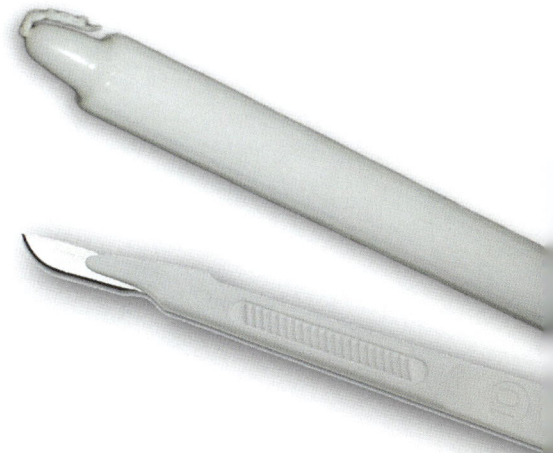

Phase 2: Project

Shabby Wooden Picture Frame

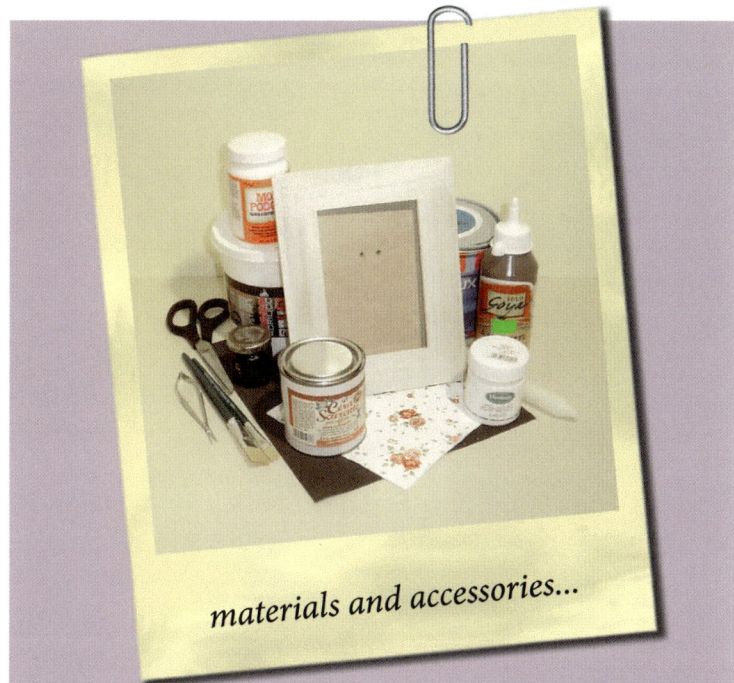

materials and accessories...

Materials

a wooden frame,
dark brown acrylic paint,
white acrylic paint,
wood primer,
napkin with a motif of roses,
paraffin,
patina,
water-based varnish and decoupage
glue.

Accessories

a scalpel,
sandpaper,
brushes and a small sponge

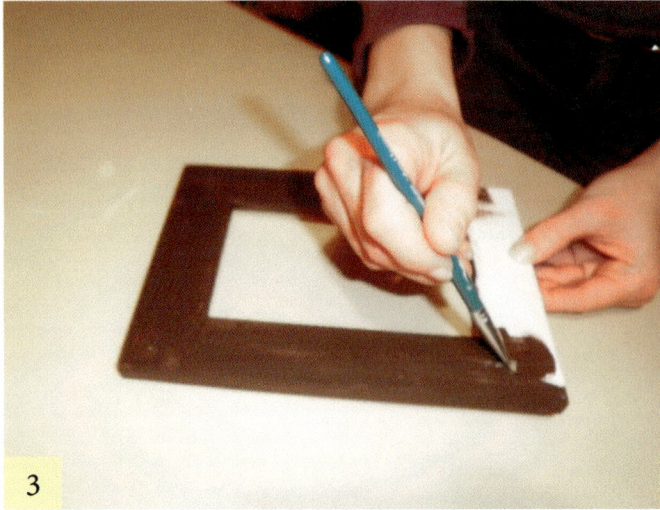

3

4

1. The wooden picture frame must first be treated with sand paper. Use paper towel to remove the dust.

2. Then it must be coated with wood primer and left to dry.

3. Apply a brown colour on the parts of the surface where your predict wear and tear or onto the entire frame. Wait for the coat of paint to dry.

4. Rub paraffin on all outer edges of the frame.

5. Completely coat the wooden picture frame in white acrylic paint with a brush.

6. Wait until the layer of white paint has dried thoroughly. Remove the white colour where needed with coarse sandpaper or a scalpel (on those places where you had previously applied the dark colour and paraffin).

7. Divide the three-layered napkin into layers - we will only use the top layer with the image. Seeing that the roses on the napkin are tiny and difficult to cut with scissors, tear out the necessary motifs with your fingers. Thanks to this technique, the edges of our motifs will fit the area provided.

5

6

8

8. Secure the selected motifs using decoupage glue. Apply the glue with a flat synthetic brush, carefully pressing the napkin from the centre towards the edges, expelling the air bubbles. Be careful because the napkin can easily tear.

9. Once the glue has dried, apply the patina using a small sponge. This is how the box gets an antique look. Be careful! If there is too much patina, the frame will look dirty. It is important to know how much to apply.

10. Once the patina has dried, apply the finishing varnish in several layers, waiting for one coat to dry before applying the next. It's best to choose glossy varnish. The picture frame is done!

It's possible to decorate a range of objects in shabby chic style in the same way: chests, candlesticks, retro wooden toys, but also larger objects like tables, dressers, etc. Any object decorated in shabby chic style will contribute to the beauty of the interior by bringing a breath of long forgotten romance.

9

after...

Phase 2: Project

Birdhouse

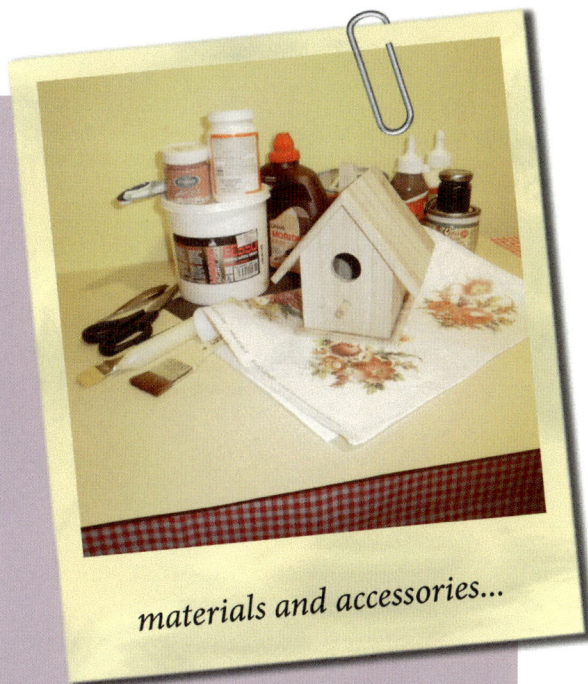

materials and accessories...

Materials

a wooden birdhouse,
floral patterned rice paper,
wood primer,
decoupage glue,
brown acrylic paint,
dirty pink acrylic paint,
white acrylic paint,
patina,
wood stain in oak colour,
paraffin and water-based varnish

Accessories

a scalpel,
sandpaper,
a toothbrush,
a small sponge and brushes

2

3

1. Before you begin decorating, first sandpaper the previously prepared box. It's best to use fine sandpaper. Wipe the surface with paper towels.

2. Paint the entire house with wood primer, except the edges of the roof and the edges of the base.

3. Paint the edges of the roof and the box opening with brown colour and rub in paraffin.

4. Completely coat the top side of the roof with white acrylic paint twice.

5. Apply a dirty pink acrylic colour on all surfaces of the birdhouse, except for the outer surface of the roof. A broad synthetic brush is the most appropriate for this task. Wait until the layer of paint has dried and then apply the next layer.

6. Stain the edges of the base. It's best to choose a shade of oak.

5

6

7

8

7. Use a scalpel to remove the white colour off the edges of the roof where you have put paraffin.

8. Sand all sides of the birdhouse using coarse sandpaper.

9. Rice paper is applied on the top of the roof. Put the floral motif from the rice paper on the surface of the birdhouse and apply the adhesive with a flat brush. Press the motif from the centre towards the edges, forcing the air bubbles out.

Surplus pieces of rice paper should be carefully removed with sandpaper before the glue has dried.

10. Spray the birdhouse with a dark brown acrylic paint using a toothbrush and a wooden stick. Repeat the process using white colour.

11. Sand all bonds on the roof once again. Tone the edges of the roof using bitumen and a sponge. Cover the birdhouse with a protective layer of transparent varnish once the work is completely dry. Done!

10

after...

Phase 1: Technique

Crackle varnish

Crackle varnish gives a fantastic antique effect in combination with napkin technique, rice paper and patina. Cracks can then be seen on motifs too, as napkins and rice paper are transparent.

It's ideal for adding an antique feel to furniture and various other decorative objects.

BOTTOM LAYER

Coat the object with a darker acrylic paint. When the acrylic paint dries, apply crackle varnish using a solid and broad brush, spread it evenly (so you're not left with a too thick layer) in one direction (left-right or up-down). NEVER apply crackle varnish on the same spot twice. Apply once, dip the brush and continue where you left of, always in the same direction.

Leave varnish to air dry, and if you want to speed up the drying process, you can warm up the varnish using a hair dryer (it's dry in a few minutes).

If left to air dry, varnish will dry in 30 minutes to an hour (depending on the temperature and humidity). If the humidity is extremely high it can take longer for the varnish to dry.

bottom layer...

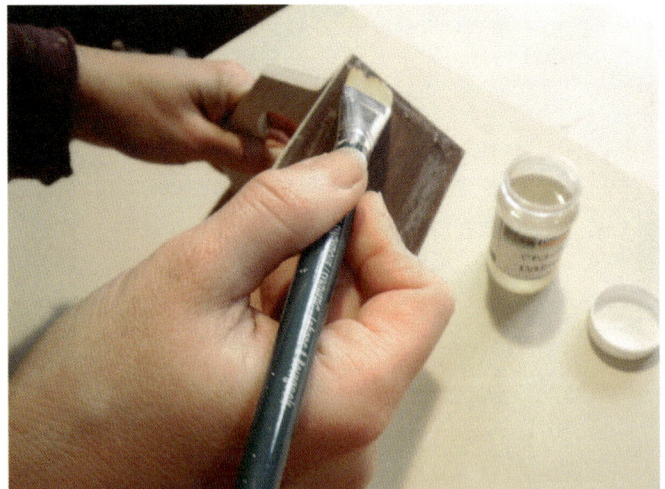

TOP LAYER

Apply a coat of bright acrylic paint on dry varnish (no longer sticky to the touch) - such as a vanilla colour. Apply the paint in one direction. Denser colour means bigger cracks. Apply the paint with a brush or even better, with a foam brush. Apply ONLY ONE layer of bright acrylic paint, because otherwise the cracks won't appear...

As the paint dries, the cracks start appearing.

The top colour doesn't have to be applied as soon as the varnish dries (the varnish doesn't lose its capacity to crack with time).

If you want, you can glue the napkin with varnish or napkin glue.

The napkin takes on a cracked appearance although it isn't cracked, because of the dark colour in the cracks.

The whole object can finally be protected with varnish or napkin glue.

top layer...

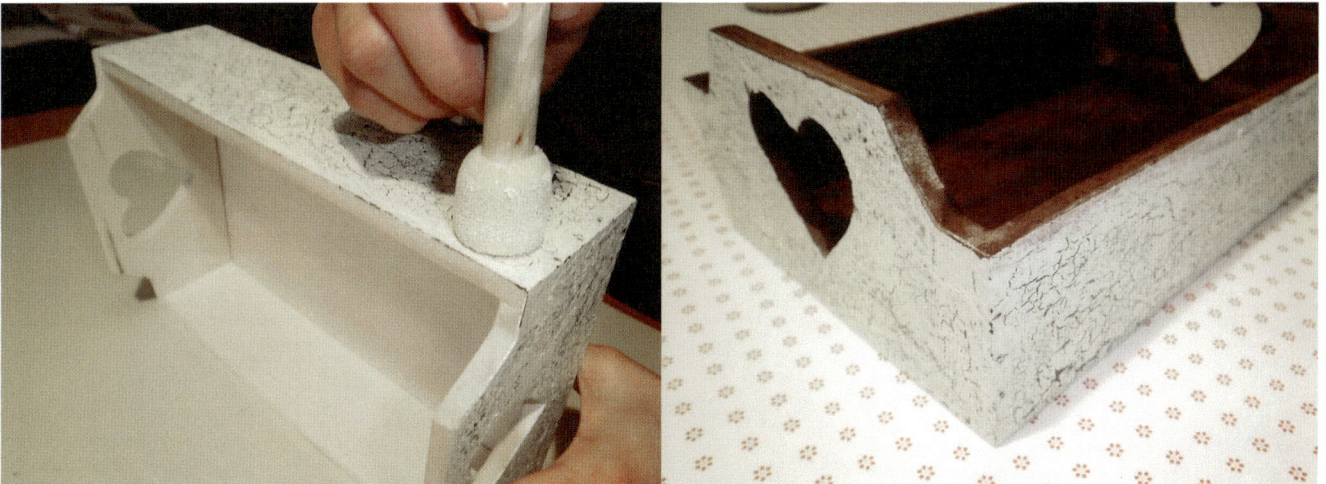

Painting on a Round Wooden Base

materials and accessories...

Materials

a round wooden base,
dark green acrylic paint,
ivory acrylic paint,
napkin with an olive motif,
crackle varnish,
patina,
wood primer,
paraffin and decoupage glue.

Accessories

brushes,
scissors,
a small sponge,
sandpaper and a foam brush.

1

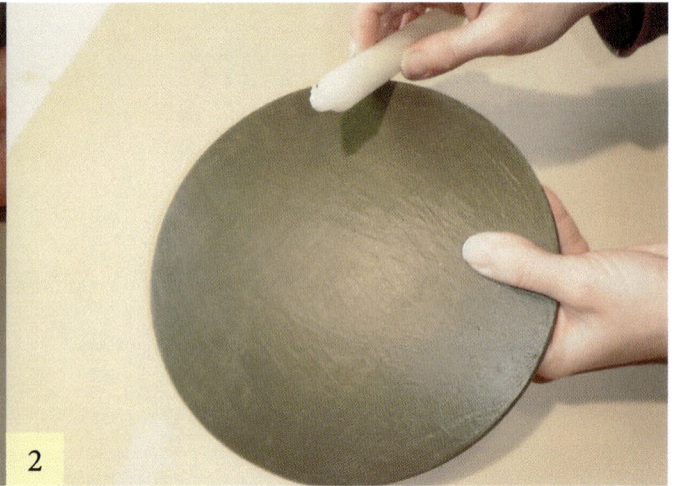

2

1. After sanding, first coat the wooden surface with wood primer.

2. Then coat the wooden base with acrylic paint, in a shade of green earth. When the paint is dry, rub the edges with paraffin.

3. Coat the middle with crackle varnish and leave to dry.

TIP !

How to achieve large cracks when working with crackle varnish?

The size of the cracks depends solely on the thickness of the upper layer of paint. If you apply this colour thinly, cracks will be small and vice versa.

It's always better to apply the upper colour by patting with a sponge or a foam brush because then you can scoop up more colour, and ugly brush strokes won't be visible, which is the biggest problem when using crackle varnish.[15]

3

---

[15]http://www.nb-net.hr/nbh6.php. (09.02.2013.).

4. When crackle varnish has dried, paint or pat the whole picture with a foam brush in a shade of ivory.

5. Cracks will appear in places where crackle varnish was applied. Using a scalpel scrape off the part where paraffin was after drying and then sand with sandpaper.

6. At the end paste the napkin using napkin glue.

after...

Phase 2: Project

Wooden Tray with Sunflowers

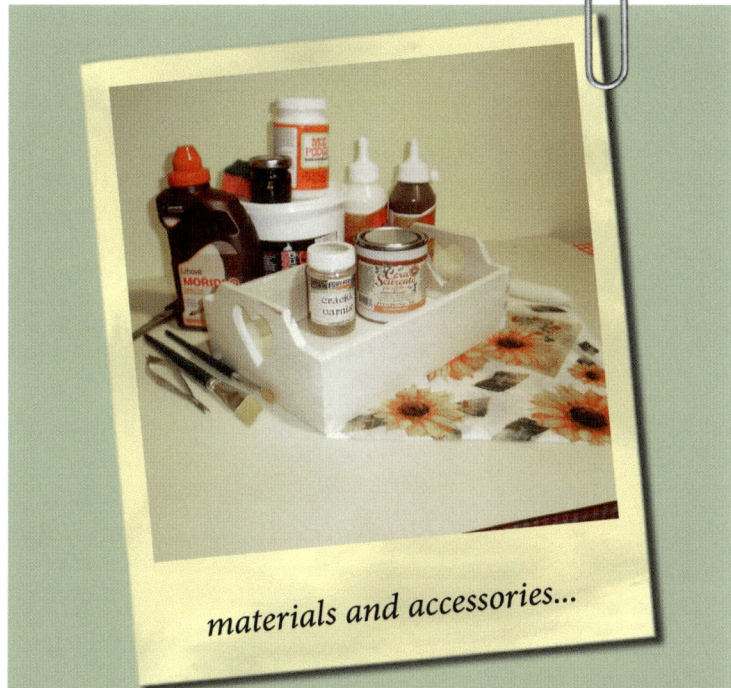

materials and accessories...

Materials

a wooden tray,
rosewood coloured stain,
brown acrylic paint,
ivory acrylic paint,
crackle varnish,
patina,
decoupage glue,
water-based varnish,
wood primer,
rice paper with sunflower motif and
paraffin.

Accessories

brushes and a small sponge,
a scalpel,
sandpaper and a foam brush.

1

3

1. Sand all surfaces of the tray using small grit sandpaper.

2. Paint the external sides of the tray with wood primer, then paint with a dark brown acrylic paint. Allow plenty of time for the paint to dry.

3. Once the paint is dry, rub the edges of the tray with paraffin; apply crackle varnish in the middle of external sides and leave to dry.

4. When crackle varnish has dried, pat all external sides of the tray with ivory acrylic paint. Use a foam brush. Cracks will appear in places where crackle varnish was applied.

5. Coat the interior of the box with rosewood coloured stain to highlight the wood structure. Wait for the wood stain to dry.

4

5

6

6. Parts rubbed with paraffin should be scraped off with a scalpel after drying and then sanded.

7. Glue the sunflower motifs with a flat brush and decoupage glue on all external sides of the tray.

8. Apply the patina on the edges of the tray using a sponge.

8

after...

Phase 1: Technique

Two-Component Crackle Varnish

Apply the paint and decoupage paper or the napkin. Apply the first phase (step1) of the two-component varnish on the dried surface and leave to dry for 30 minutes and not longer. The varnish is white and will cover the surface, but becomes translucent after drying. The first phase may not be applied in a thick layer, but must be applied everywhere.

Apply the second phase of crackle varnish (step 2) abundantly using a dry flat brush. Cracks will appear after drying.

To emphasize the cracks, rub oil paint, bitumen or porporino in them. Excess paint, tar or powder can be wiped off with a cloth after rubbing in order to get the samples, i.e., cracks where we want them. Two-component varnish becomes glossy after drying and it does not have to be lacquered over.

Wooden Box for Sewing Accessories

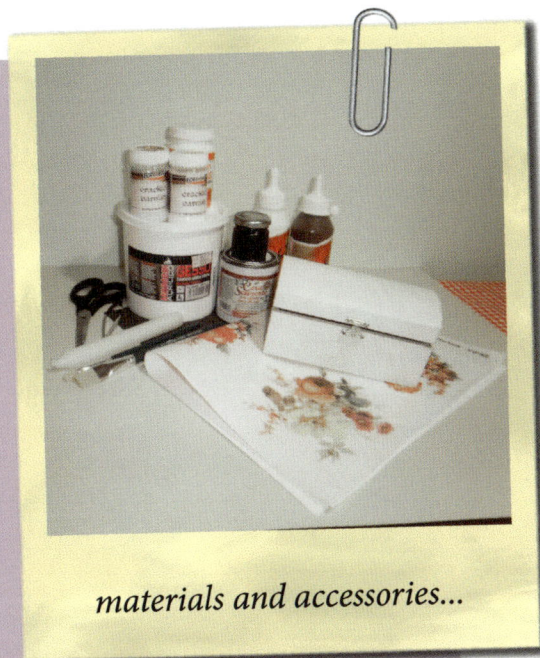

materials and accessories...

Materials

a wooden box,
brown acrylic paint,
ivory acrylic paint,
two-component crackle varnish,
patina,
decoupage glue,
rice paper with floral pattern,
wood primer and paraffin.

Accessories

brushes,
scalpel,
a small sponge,
scissors,
sandpaper and a thin cotton cloth.

1

5

TIP !

When using a patina, always wear disposable protective gloves, because patina is not water-based. Simply put the gloves on and take a piece of an old linen cloth. Dispose of both gloves and cloth when done. That's how you'll avoid cleaning your hands with thinner.[16]

1. Sand the box using sandpaper.

2. Coat all outer sides of the box and the lid with wood primer.

3. Paint the edges of the box and the lid with dark brown acrylic paint. Rub paraffin on all outer edges of the box and the lid to give them an antique look.

4. Apply the ivory acrylic paint on the outside of the box using a sponge. Allow plenty of time for the paint to dry.

5. Scrape the outer edges of the box and the lid with a scalpel (where you rubbed with paraffin).

6. Cut the selected floral motifs from rice paper into bits using scissors.

7. Stick rice paper motifs on the box using a flat brush and decoupage glue.

[16]http://www.lumos.hr/ideje.htm. (09.02.2013.).

9

10

8. Apply the first layer of two-component crackle varnish on the parts of the box plastered with floral motifs from rice paper. Wait 30 minutes for the coat to dry. Keep in mind that the size of the cracks depends on the thickness of the applied coat of varnish.

9. Apply the second layer of two-component crackle varnish using a flat brush. Wait 30-40 minutes for the layer to dry. After the cracks have formed rub bitumen in them. It's best to use a thin lint-free cotton cloth.

10. Tone the edges of the lid with bitumen.

11. The wooden box already has a high gloss, so it's not necessary to apply the finishing varnish.

after...

Phase 2: Project

Antique Metal Jug

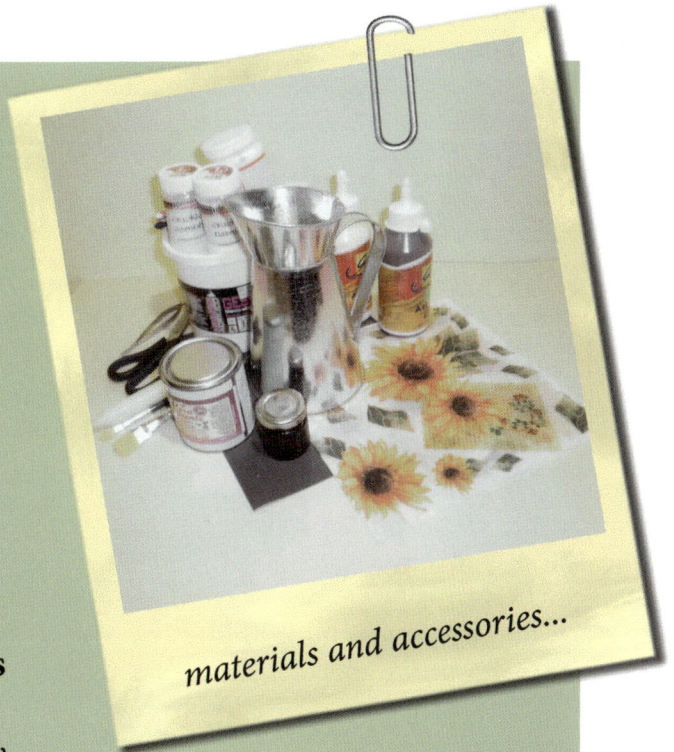

materials and accessories...

Materials

a metal jug,
metal primer,
brown acrylic paint,
ivory acrylic paint,
decoupage glue,
rice paper depicting sunflowers,
patina,
two-component crackle varnish and
paraffin.

Accessories

brushes,
sponges,
a scalpel,
scissors and a thin cotton cloth.

1. Before you start decorating, it's necessary to check whether the metal jug is damaged. If it is, fill the defects with putty. Wait for the putty to dry thoroughly. Apply metal primer in two layers to the surface of the pitcher, waiting for the first coat to dry thoroughly before applying the second.

2. Coat the edges of the jug with a dark brown colour and rub them with paraffin.

3. Coat the jug with acrylic ivory colour. This colour is also applied in two layers. Before applying the second coat it's necessary to wait for the first coat to dry thoroughly.

4. Choose rice paper with an appropriate sunflower motif. Cut motifs (do not tear, because in this case we need a straight edge of the image).

5. Carefully stick the rice paper onto the metal jug using decoupage glue. To paste the rice paper it's best to use a soft brush, and to press the paper from the centre towards the edges, avoiding the formation of wrinkles. It's especially important to press the ends so they don't come off later.

5

9

6. Apply the first layer of two-component crackle varnish onto the metal jug covered in sunflower motifs from rice paper. Wait 30 minutes for the coat to dry. Keep in mind that the size of the cracks depends on the thickness of the applied coat of varnish.

7. Apply the second layer of two-component crackle varnish using a flat brush. Wait 30-40 minutes for the layer to dry. After the cracks have formed rub bitumen in them. It's best to use a thin lint-free cotton cloth.

8. Scrape the outer edges of the pitcher with a scalpel (where you rubbed with paraffin).

9. Apply patina onto the edges of the jar using a sponge. This is a way to isolate the protruding elements or components that wear out faster (handles, edges, etc.).

10. Metal pitcher already has a high gloss, so it's not necessary to apply the finishing varnish.

after...

Phase 1: Technique

Staining Wood

Staining or soaking is a technique of painting or changing the colour and protecting the natural wood at the same time.

By staining we achieve transparent wood protection, which means that under the protective colour coat, which adheres well to wood and penetrates it deeply, rings and wood structure are visible. Acrylic protective wood coating can be diluted with water and penetrates even hard wood such as ash, beech and oak well. This procedure changes or refreshes the existing wood colour.

In order to better absorb the stain into the wood, it's necessary to remove grease and dirt from it. Once it's dry, wood should first be roughly sanded, and then more finely, until the last treatment with sandpaper marked 200.

TIP !

Patina gives objects an antique look. It works great on a white background because it's transparent, while it doesn't look so good on pastel colours. If you use a single component patina then apply it with a cloth and let it dry.

If you use colour and oil for patination, then first mix the components in proportions specified on the packaging and apply the patina in the same way as the previous one. Patina is not water-based so always clean your hands with thinner.[16]

Patina is ideal to apply on varnished wood because it gives wood a touch of history and a warm brown colour, highlighting the wood structure and the tree rings...

Besides liquid preparations, coloured powder, which is easily and quickly absorbed into even new wood after coating, can be used for staining.

When the staining fluid is ready to use, a powder is blended into it. The stain can dissolve in tap water or in a mixture of water and alcohol, with higher ratio of water giving a brighter hue. Stains adhere well to skin, as well as wood, so it's necessary to use protective garments, such as rubber gloves. Staining wood is done with a sponge, brush or roller, so that the surface is as wet as can be and in the direction of wood grain, spreading the stain evenly.

Phase 2: Project

Wooden Box for Napkin Holders

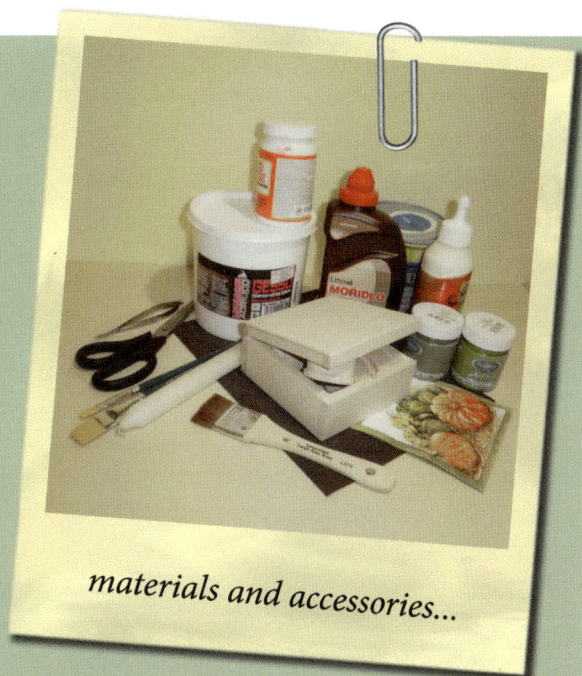

materials and accessories...

Materials

a wooden box,
oak coloured stain,
wood primer,
white acrylic paint,
green acrylic paint,
patina, napkin with a zucchini motif,
decoupage glue,
water-based varnish and paraffin.

Accessories

brushes,
sandpaper,
a sponge and a toothbrush.

2

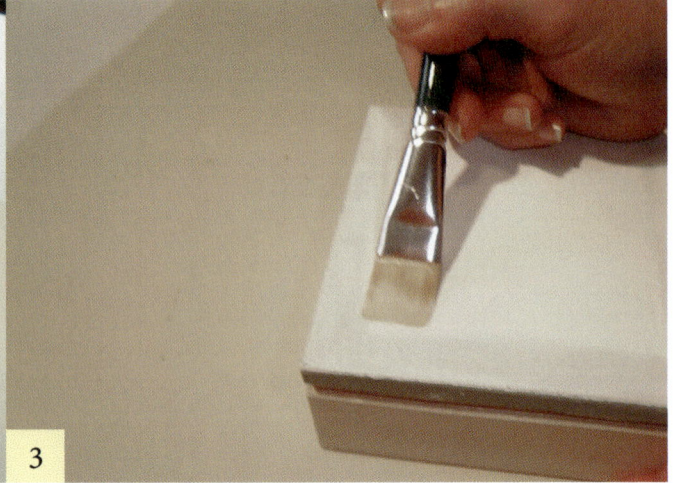

3

1. Carefully coat the spot where you'll attach the motif with wood primer. We will prevent wood layering in this manner, and therefore the image won't be deformed.

2. Apply a beautiful green coloured acrylic paint on a flat dry brush. Tone top and side edges of the lid, and rub them with paraffin.

3. Coat the top of the lid with white acrylic paint.

4. Stain the inside and the outside of the box and napkin holders with oak coloured stain. Allow the stained surface enough time to dry.

5. Set the napkin motif, previously painting the surface with decoupage glue. The top picture should also be painted with decoupage glue, avoiding the formation of bubbles or tearing of the napkin.

6. The edges of the napkin should not look too accurate, but should be carefully sanded in case we need to apply glue once again.

4

8

9

7. The surfaces will appear "antique" by sanding. It's best to use sandpaper with fine grit.

8. Make dots using a toothbrush. It's necessary to apply a dark brown colour onto the toothbrush, and then spray the upper surface of the box by stroking the tooth brush "towards yourself." Wait for the dark colour to dry. Repeat the process using the white colour.

9. Tone the edges of the box with bitumen using a sponge.

10. Coat the lid with a final layer of acrylic varnish. It's best to choose a varnish with a matte effect. The box for napkin holders is done!

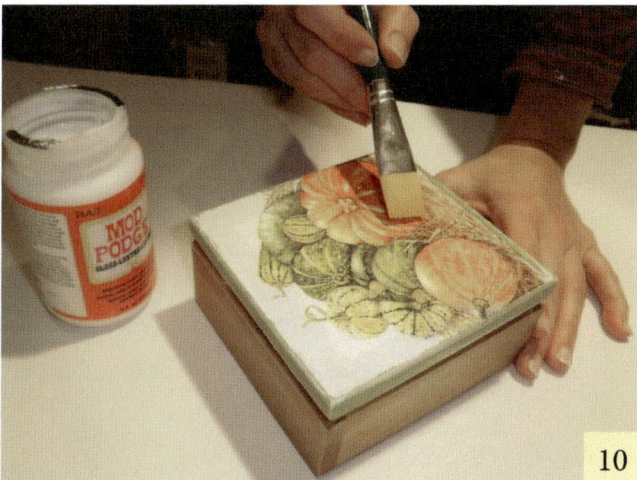

10

after...

Phase 2: Project

Wooden Bread Box

materials and accessories...

Materials

a wooden box,
wood primer,
ivory acrylic paint,
brown acrylic paint,
decoupage glue,
a napkin with chestnut motif,
patina,
paraffin,
oak coloured stain and water-based
varnish.

Accessories

brushes,
sponges,
a toothbrush,
a scalpel,
sandpaper and scissors.

1. Before you start decorating, it's necessary to check whether the wooden box is damaged. If it is, fill the defects with wood putty. Wait for the putty to dry thoroughly. Apply wood primer to the outer sides of the box.

2. Stain the interior of the box with oak coloured stain.

3. Coat the outer edges of the box with a dark brown acrylic colour and rub them with paraffin.

4. Coat all outer sides with ivory acrylic colour. This colour is also applied in two layers. Before applying the second coat it's necessary to wait for the first coat to dry thoroughly.

5. Scrape all outer edges of the box with a scalpel.

6. Choosing a napkin with an appropriate motif of a chestnut. Cut motifs (do not tear, because in this case we need a straight edge of the image) and separate the layers of the napkin. We will need only its upper, colourful layer.

7. Carefully stick the chestnut motif onto the box using decoupage glue. To paste the napkin it's best to use a soft brush, and then press the paper from the centre towards the edges, avoiding the formation of wrinkles. It's especially important to press the ends so they don't come off later.

9

10

8. Make dots using a toothbrush. It's necessary to apply a dark brown colour onto the toothbrush, and then spray the upper surface of the box by stroking the toothbrush "towards yourself" (this is important, because if we spray "away from ourselves", paint drops will fly into our eyes). Wait for the dark colour to dry.

9. Repeat the process using the white colour. Don't hesitate to spray over the chestnut motif – the box will only look better.

10. Apply patina to the edges of the box using a sponge.

11. After patina is dry, protect the decoration. Coat all exterior surfaces with acrylic varnish. Apply a minimum of two coats, waiting for each coat to dry before applying the next. Our kitchen wooden box is finished! If you want, you can decorate kitchen furniture, table and chairs, and even your grandmother's antique cabinet using the same technique and colour palette.

11

after...

Phase 1: Technique

Working with Structural Paste, Stencils and Stamps

Structural paste is used for achieving relief and volume on various surfaces. It's used on surfaces such as canvases, wooden objects, MDF, etc...

Structural pastes are divided into two groups, pastes and gels. They are both high density acrylic pastes used for 3D effects and adding structure in various techniques. Pastes cover the surface and become opaque after drying, while gels become transparent after drying. All pastes are applied with spatulas which should be rinsed with water after use.[18]

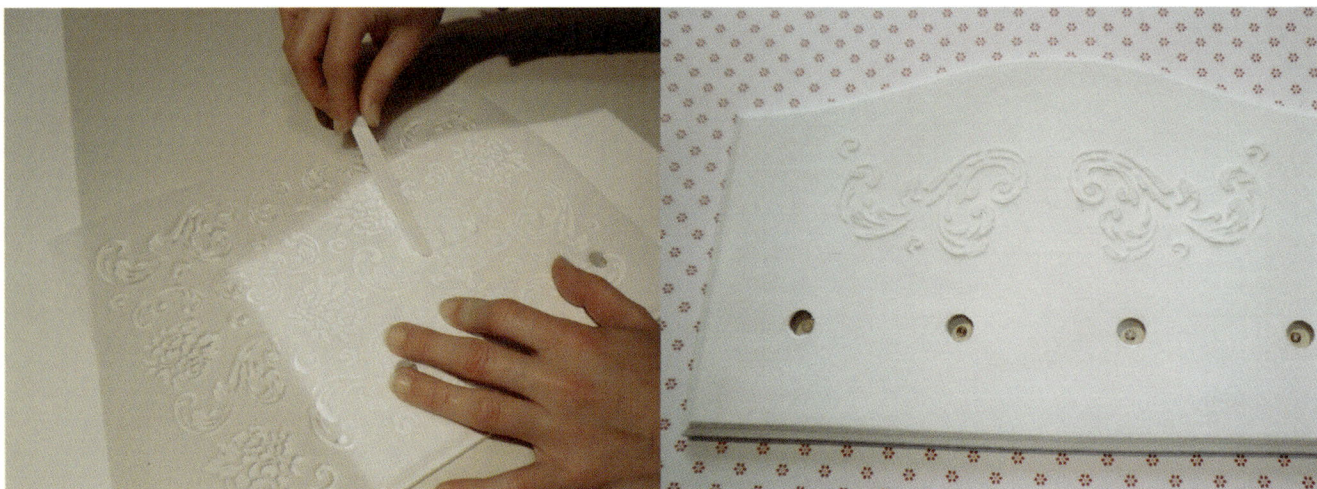

---

[18]Data in the Section on Working with Structural Paste, Stencils and Stamps is taken from http://www.lumos.hr/strukturneboje.htm. (20.02.2013.).

Stamps and stencils

Using stamps and stencils for creative projects has become very popular in recent years.

Stamps

All you really need is a stamp and a little colour. Stamps can be bought in arts and crafts stores. These are mostly rubber or silicone stamps with smaller motifs for use in making greeting cards or scrapbooking. You must also get ink pads that come in various colours.[19]

Stencils

As well as stamps, stencils can be bought ready-made and ready to use. The difference between stamps and stencils is that a stencil is actually a negative of an image or a text, which is attached to the surface of the object we want to embellish, and then colour which remains after drying is applied on it.

Stencils are usually made from thin sheets of plastic, and there are also self-adherent stencils which prevent the paint from "leaking" out of them. These plastic stencils can be reused.[20]

Place the stencil on the desired surface, such as a box, picture frame or a greeting card. Secure it well and apply the colour, best using a foam brush. Make sure the paint doesn't leak. Remove the template after drying. And that's it...

[19]Data in the Section on Working with Structural Paste, Stencils and Stamps http://www.kutijica.net/category/tehnike/upotreba-pecata-i-sablona-tehnike/. (20.02.2013.).
[20]Data in the Section on Working with Structural Paste, Stencils and Stamps http://www.kutijica.net/category/tehnike/upotreba-pecata-i-sablona-tehnike/. (20.02.2013.).

Phase 2: Project

Shabby Chic Hanger

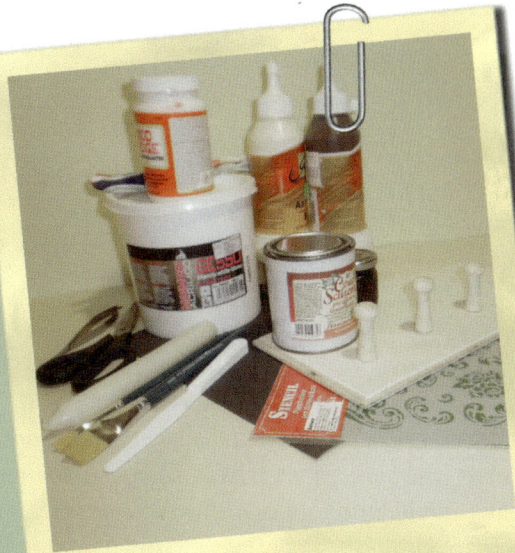

materials and accessories...

Materials

a wooden hanger,
a stencil,
structural paste,
wood primer,
dark brown acrylic paint,
acrylic paint in a light beige shade,
patina and paraffin.

Accessories

a plastic knife,
brushes,
a sponge,
a scalpel,
a toothbrush and sandpaper.

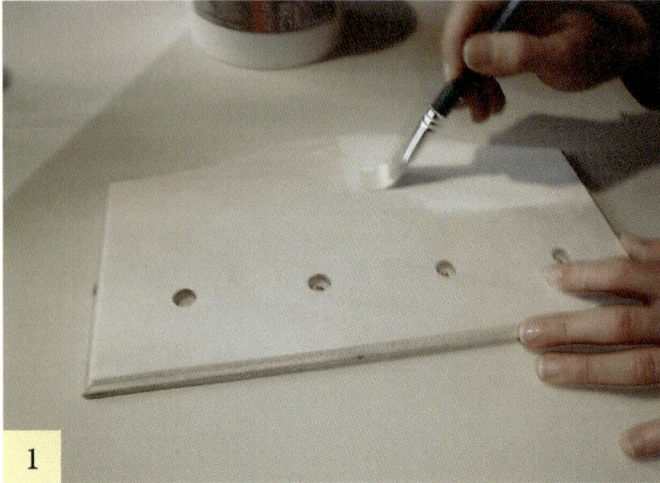

1. It's necessary to sand the surface of the wooden hanger with fine sandpaper first. Use paper towels to remove dust, then apply wood primer. It's important to think of the design in advance.

2. Place the stencil on the desired spot. Apply a thick layer of structural paste over the stencil using a knife. Remove the stencil carefully and leave enough time for the paste to fully dry.

3. Once the paste has dried, apply a dark brown acrylic paint on all surfaces of the hanger. It's best to use a broad synthetic brush.

4. Let the paint dry. Rub paraffin on the spots on the hanger where you plan to imitate peeling. Remove the excessive bits of wax.

5. Coat the entire hanger with a light beige shade of acrylic paint. This coat should not be too thick.

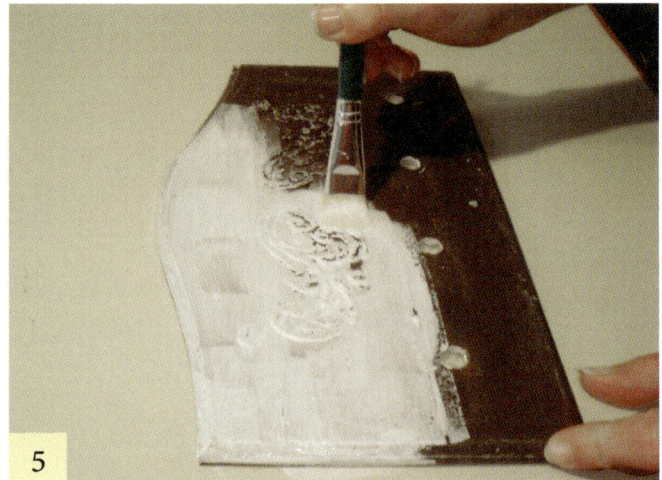

8

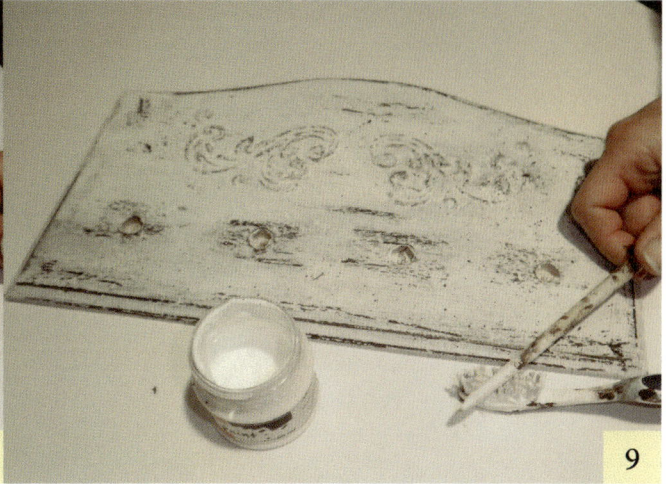

9

6. Once the paint is dry, sand the areas that have been previously rubbed with paraffin. It's best to use medium grit sandpaper. Remove only the layer of beige. If the dark brown coat comes off too, it's a sign that the paint is not dry yet. In places where we've applied wax, the colour will come off and the brown background will be visible.

7. Paint the hooks in the same manner as the board and attach them to the board.

8. Using a toothbrush and a wooden stick, spray the hanger with dark acrylic paint.

9. Repeat the process using a light colour.

10. Apply patina on the edges of the stencil using a sponge (to emphasize the 3D effect) and to the edges of the board to age the hanger.

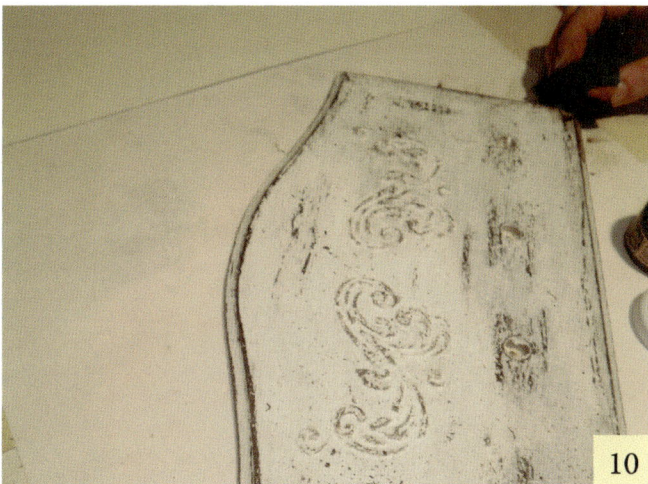

10

after...

Phase 2: Project

Romantic Clock

materials and accessories...

Materials

an MDF base for the clock,
clockwork and hands,
wood primer,
neutral colourless wax,
a silicone stamp,
a stencil,
floral patterned rice paper,
a pale green shade of acrylic paint,
black acrylic paint,
ivory acrylic paint,
dark brown acrylic paint,
mushroom coloured acrylic paint,
patina,
a stencil with numbers and letters
and decoupage glue

Accessories

brushes,
a sponge,
sandpaper and
a phantom pen

1. Paint the surface of the clock with white primer and let it dry.

2. Choose a pale shade of green acrylic paint and ivory colour and pour a small amount in the container for mixing colours. Take a small amount of every hue with a sponge and pat all over the surface of the clock.

3. Then coat the entire surface with neutral colourless wax which will give it a satin sheen, smell wonderful and make the surface more slippery for the next layer of paint.

4. Trace around the border of the inner clock circle using a phantom pen.

5. Paint the inner circle with black paint. Leave it to dry.

6. Sand the interior of the clock circle painted black with medium grit sandpaper.

7. Take the stencil and place it on the outside of the base and gently transfer the pattern with a foam brush dipped in diluted mushroom colour, so that there is only a shadow left.

8. Choose stamps you like and apply them using a sponge dipped in mushroom acrylic paint and stamp the inside of the clock coated in black.

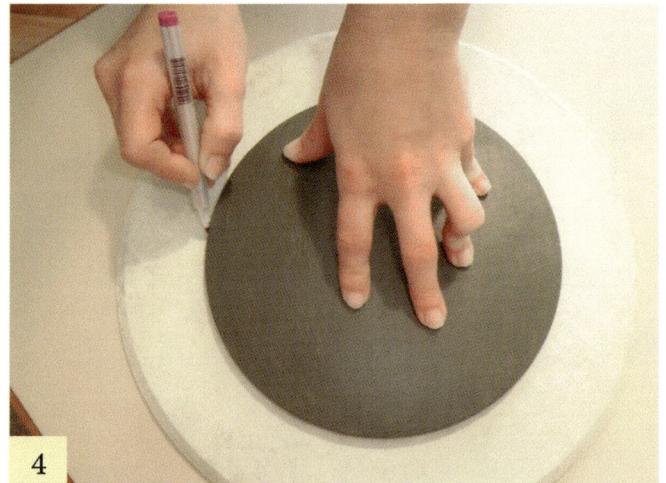

5

7

9. Take the stencil with numbers and letters and lightly transfer numbers and letters to desired positions using a sponge dipped in ivory colour.

10. Draw tiny dots on the interior edge of the clock using a thin brush, in the same colour as numbers and letters.

11. Choose the rice paper with an appropriate motif. Tear out the motifs from the rice paper.

12. Carefully stick rice paper motifs on the outer border of the clock.

13. Tone the edges of the clock with bitumen.

14. Coat the clock with neutral colourless wax using a sponge.

13

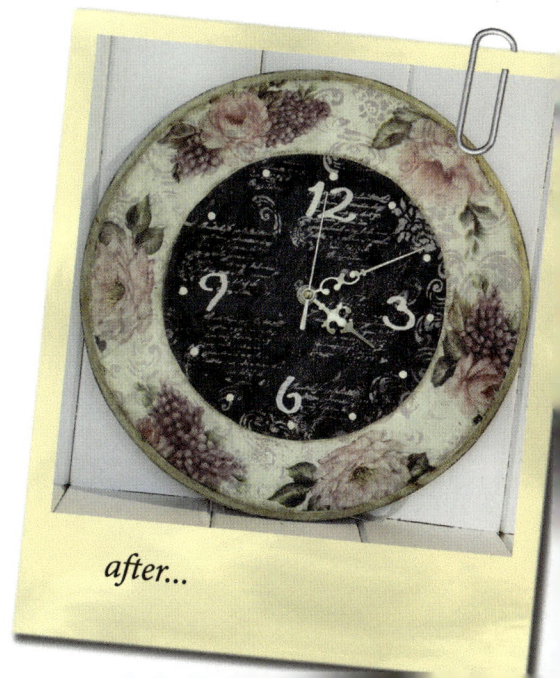

after...

INDEX

Sources

http://www.lumos.hr
http://www.nb-net.hr/
http://www.perlica.hr/
http://www.hobbyart-chemaco.hr/
http://www.artshop.hr/
http://hobbyboom.blogspot.com
http://hobbychic.blogspot.com/
http://www.kutijica.net/

My favourite blogs and websites on decoupage

http://marinanikulina.blogspot.com/
http://hobbychic.blogspot.com/
http://biljanashabby.blogspot.com/
http://mare-ri.blogspot.com/
http://pasjadecoupage.pl
http://asket.blox.pl

I thank the sponsors for their generous support in finishing this book!

Printed in Great Britain
by Amazon.co.uk, Ltd.,
Marston Gate.